ANCHOR BOOKS

CREATION'S DAWN

Edited by

Kelly Deacon

First published in Great Britain in 2000 by
ANCHOR BOOKS
Remus House,
Coltsfoot Drive,
Woodston,
Peterborough, PE2 9JX
Telephone (01733) 898102

HB ISBN 1 85930 810 4
SB ISBN 1 85930 815 5

FOREWORD

There are many reasons why people turn to the written form, perhaps as a form of relief or a way to express one's feelings. A lot of the time it is a tragedy or some form of celebration that inspires a person to put pen to paper. Often people, friends and family, pets, hobbies and places, lend themselves as a subject on which to centre our poetry.

However, *Creation's Dawn* is a little different. All the poets in this collection were presented a challenge - to write a poem to the very specific styles of the villanelle and sonnet. Each poet has a different story to tell or message to spread - however they have risen to the challenge with vigour and excellence.

So sit back and allow this inspiring poetic form to fill your mind, become one with not only the written word but the villanelle and sonnet as well.

Kelly Deacon
Editor

CONTENTS

THE WEDDING NIGHT

I am the river that flows through the town,
Why do you come so late and alone?
Don't enter my body you'll surely drown.

My waters are staining your ivory gown;
Trees overhead wave branches that moan:
I am the river that flows through the town.

My waters are cold, deep and brown;
His name you whisper, a repeating drone:
Don't enter my body you'll surely drown.

Your pure face is sad, without a frown,
He married another but his heart you still own:
I am the river that flows through the town.

His bride is a princess she gave him a crown;
From the site of the wedding to me you have flown:
Don't enter my body you'll surely drown.

I feel you stumbling, tumbling down,
After tonight he won't care for his throne:
I am the river that flows through the town,
Don't enter my body you'll surely drown.

A M Barwani

EMOTIONS

Waves splashing over pebbles on the shore
No longer in love, young and carefree
A tide of emotions washed away for evermore

Such perfection in my eyes, no single flaw
Why did you have to marry me?
Waves splashing over pebbles on the shore

Expectations of a future with happiness galore
No longer lasting forever you see
A tide of emotions washed away for evermore

My heart got broken my feelings left raw
Another woman turned two into three
Waves splashing over pebbles on the shore

You left when I showed you the door
Why did you prefer her to me?
A tide of emotions washed away for evermore

Settlement made in a court of law
Now just another statistic, a lone divorcee
Waves splashing over pebbles on the shore
A tide of emotions washed away for evermore.

Sally Vale

CAPITULATION

Warm, tranquil, glorious August evening,
Crowning a memorable summer's day.
Still shadows dimming the hillside greening,
The valley lake reflects the sun's last ray.
The mystical moon, with blue eerie light,
Transforms the rough grass on which we both lie.
Tomorrow, when the fickle sun shines bright,
Across the miles, remember and hear me sigh.
For now you speak with words full of feeling
And I rebuke you, moody in response.
I shiver at your touch, senses reeling,
Passion surges with desire, to ensconce.

Sinews sing, straining for your male embrace,
Repressed love accepts, with gentle grace.

Mabel McCoy

YELLOW PERIL

My garden's full of daffodils
Each border is a-groan with them
And so are my window sills.
The sea of yellow flows and spills
Around, about each stalk and stem
My garden's full of daffodils
Up to their ears in yellow frills
The garden's quite an anadem
And so are all my window sills.
Not narcissi, no - nor jonquils
Or flowers as dignified as them -
My garden's full of daffodils.
Each tidy border overspills -
Blazing with ochre meristem
And so are all my window sills.
The twentieth vase, this armful fills
I shall not plant this bulb again!
My garden's full of daffodils
And so are all my window sills.

Lal Asharni

VILLANELLE WRITTEN ON A FARM

From here I miss the daily ebb and flow,
Though leaves unfurl and birds arrive with spring,
I cannot see the cold sea come and go.

I walk by paths through fields and woods and though,
I love the calm embrace the trees can bring,
From here I miss the daily ebb and flow.

Before, a glance down to the straits would show,
The flood, the ebb, the slack, the state of things,
Now I can't see the cold sea come and go.

I need to set my clock by time less slow,
Than growing buds and leaves, than birds that sing,
From here I miss the daily ebb and flow.

It comforts me to watch the moon and know,
By its bright face if we're at neaps or springs,
But I can't see the cold sea come and go.

I *will* return, once more the wind will blow
Me free before my feet take root and cling.
From here I miss the daily ebb and flow,
I cannot see the cold sea come and go.

Tim Rogers

VILLANELLE FOR VIRGINIA

When Virginia Woolf comes round to tea,
We skip conventional talk per se,
Our narratives flow deep and free.

We drink a brew of Bloomsbury,
Crumble rules and snap cliché,
When Virginia Woolf comes round to tea.

We voyage out upon a sea
Of images, purer than the day.
Our narratives flow deep and free

And plunge us into complexity.
Our thoughts spread out like a bouquet,
When Virginia Woolf comes round to tea,

They perfume the room with reverie
And tinge the walls with a purple spray.
Our narratives flow deep and free.

An Angel in the House is she,
She lets introspection out to play.
When Virginia Woolf comes round to tea,
Our narratives flow deep and free.

Jennifer Howe

VILLANELLE

Drink too much and you risk being banned
To trade your health for a gallon of booze,
It may be more than a poor man can stand.

So divert yourself and play in a band
Or astound your wife by replacing that fuse,
Drink too much and you risk being banned.

Take the kids sailing or walk on the sand
Paint the spare bedroom in fabulous hues,
It may be more than a poor man can stand.

Adopt a near neighbour and give him a hand
'Tis there for the taking you have to choose,
Drink too much and you risk being banned.

Forget all those headaches stay un-canned
There is all to be gained and more to lose,
It may be more than a poor man can stand.

If you wager your life, play the wrong hand
Your future could be in the hands of the screws,
Drink too much and you risk being banned
It may be more than a poor man can stand.

Catherine Anne McGuinness

CALLIOPE WEAVE YOUR SPELL

Villanelle, well, well
Let's see if we can write one
Calliope weave your spell

The words just, well, fell
On the page, this could be fun
Villanelle, well, well

Verses writ, shall I revel
Tut, that's not quite done
Calliope weave your spell

Furrowed brows of muse tell
A story has begun
Villanelle, well, well

It ends where, who can tell
We wonder, wondrous one
Calliope weave your spell

We bring our muse before you, bell
Your kind peal of well done,
Villanelle, well, well
Calliope weave your spell.

Martin Harris Parry

SKIBBEREEN

There, pity wept for all that might have been,
for young and old who saw their dreams decay
as famine cast her shroud on Skibbereen.

And there, as death's chill shadow cloaked the scene,
they tried to hide their fears and knelt to pray.
There, pity wept for all that might have been.

There fever's poison occupied unseen
the crowded homes where starving people lay
as famine cast her shroud on Skibbereen.

And there, within the graveyard, lay obscene
and wasted bodies cast in disarray.
There, pity wept for all that might have been
as famine cast her shroud on Skibbereen.

Brian G D'Arcy

OBEDIENCE

These minds are circuit boards with tangled wire
Implanted underneath each shaven head
But conscience is not programmed or for hire.

A post-genetic infrastructure higher
Than a clone or sampled DNA said
These minds are circuit boards with tangled wire

Where strange commotions in the brain conspire
With fuse and solder. Bulletins are read
But conscience is not programmed or for hire.

Mixed chemical reactions drip to fire
And journeys end when childhood goes to bed,
These minds are circuit boards with tangled wire

Where blind obedience is the loudest crier
And all rebellion has been left for dead
But conscience is not programmed or for hire.

The magazines still advertise with flyers
For candidates to be perfect . . . instead,
These minds are circuit boards with tangled wire
But conscience is not programmed or for hire.

Thom Osmond

FULL MOON

The twinkling stars just fade away,
Each constellation disappears,
The full moon makes it bright as day.

Orion and the Milky Way
Slipping into a vale of tears,
The twinkling stars just fade away.

The Pole Star had its role to play,
Its going magnifies our fears,
The full moon makes it bright as day.

Where are we now? We cannot say,
Our bearings going as it clears,
The twinkling stars just fade away.

The sky is changed from dark to grey,
It is as if the dawning nears,
The full moon makes it bright as day.

The heavens no longer hold their sway,
God's glory fades as moonlight sears,
The twinkling stars just fade away,
The full moon makes it bright as day.

Patrick Davies

UNTITLED

All rivers flow into the sea,
Salmon return to where they were spawn,
My God shall reign eternally.

The clouds rain down, it's meant to be,
A baby in the tree was born,
All rivers flow into the sea.

The world is changing constantly,
The rhino's demise is because of its horn,
My God shall reign eternally.

All things are as they are created to be,
The darkness is replaced by dawn,
All rivers flow into the sea,

I'll talk to God and He with me,
He made the stars and fields of corn,
My God shall reign eternally.

Take my life and let it be,
Happy and not by life's ills forlorn,
All rivers flow into the sea,
My God shall reign eternally.

Richard Shurey

COME AND TALK CRIED THE HAWK

Come and talk, cried the hawk, where metals boil
      in the beginning, in the molten wet womb.
I shuffled off, like Hamlet, the electric coil.

And in my innocent running to my mortal brass toil
      I heard the clank of iron in the tomb.
Come and talk, cried the hawk, where metals boil.

And for the molten dead, in their graves, I coined
      the metal waters and stamped the minty loam.
I shuffled off, like Hamlet, the electric coil.

Common as muck in the wood could I but soil
      my immortal wound, cut to my mortal bone?
Come and talk, cried the hawk, where metals boil.

The sky opened like an eyelid and a surgeon soiled
      my wounded side where I wantonly roamed.
I shuffled off, like Hamlet, the electric coil.

Now my death was seven wars old as I toiled
      for good luck in my lucky lopsided room.
Come and talk, cried the hawk, where metals boil.
      I shuffled off, like Hamlet, the electric coil.

Evan Gwyn Williams

POTATO GRID

Do not wreck waffles with a smear of jam.
Or else, my love, I'll have to disappear;
My bags I'll pack, the door I'll slam.

Yes, mint sauce is quite good on tender lamb;
You've kept this habit up for half a year.
Do not wreck waffles with a smear of jam.

And parsley cream goes well with boiled ham;
But coq au vin does *not* improve with beer -
My bags I'll pack, the door I'll slam.

Your brain must lack four megabytes of RAM;
- They're not *that* burnt! The spud is not black *here!*
Do not wreck waffles with a smear of jam.

You go on, like you couldn't give a damn;
But now I'll make my ultimatum clear:
My bags I'll pack, the door I'll slam.

Conversions weld your eyes, your oiled hands cram -
I've half a mind to cauliflower your ear.
My bags I'll pack, the door I'll slam -
Do not wreck waffles with a smear of jam.

Karl Sadil

THE TURNING OF THE YEAR

The year is turning once again
The evenings are growing lighter,
Whilst lover's old springtime refrain

Sings sweetly in soft April rain,
Making each day so much brighter.
The year is turning once again

There's summer's madness to attain,
So come, hold each other tighter.
Whilst lover's old springtime refrain

Sings in the blood, through every vein,
Of love, the great disquieter.
The year is turning once again

Whilst passions last, sweet is the pain,
As extolled by every writer,
Whilst lover's old springtime refrain

Sings to his love, oh please remain,
Kisses softly to delight her,
The year is turning once again
Sing lover's old springtime refrain.

Valerie McKinley

I CANNOT TAKE IT ANYMORE

The waves are knocking on the shore
Over and over again
I cannot take it anymore

A terrible aching at my core
Is living life in vain?
The waves are knocking on the shore

Is there no sunshine at love's door?
Just cold and beating rain?
I cannot take it anymore

I'm letting out a desperate roar
Am I going insane?
The waves are knocking on the shore

Everything seems such a bore
I'm weighed down by a chain
I cannot take it anymore

I'm bleeding out of every pore
My heart in extreme pain
The waves are knocking on the shore
I cannot take it anymore

Rianne

A LEAVING VILLANELLE

Your hate-filled eyes still shout at me,
As I sink into a troubled dream.
The burning anger's plain to see.

Yesterday, you were my future key,
Shining bright our horizons seem.
Your hate-filled eyes still shout at me.

Sitting stiff-backed we drink our tea,
With shaking hands I pour the cream.
The burning anger's plain to see.

Swept along you don't hear my plea,
My cracked ice tears become a stream.
Your hate-filled eyes still shout at me.

You begged me then to set you free,
But what happened to us I scream.
Your hate-filled eyes still shout at me.
The burning anger's plain to see.

B Webster

SUSPENDED

As we woke and listened to each other's breath,
We sensed the words before they were spoken
When snow fell and stilled the motions of the earth.

Across smothered fields, lit with sun, a wreath
Of peat smoke rose like some scented beacon
As we woke and listened to each other's breath.

Pheasants left faded footprints on the path
To the wood where rigid limbs lay broken
When snow fell and stilled the motions of the earth.

Along the floor, a shadow moved like a wraith
And I felt your arms around me weaken
As we woke and listened to each other's breath.

No reflected flames unsettled the hearth,
Unswept ashes slowly chill and deepen
When snow fell and stilled the motions of the earth.

In love's suspension between birth and death,
We drew together with each breath taken
As we woke and listened to each other's breath
When snow fell and stilled the motions of the earth.

James K Whittet

MADAME DU DEFFAND TO HORACE WALPOLE

This is the letter that I should not write
For reading it you would be mortified.
Am I so cloying, clinging, in your sight?

My blindness renders day as dark as night.
Only in dreams I see you at my side.
This is the letter that I should not write.

Must you withdraw in chagrin, feel I slight
Your sensibilities, love's name deride?
Am I so cloying, clinging, in your sight?

If you, like me, no longer looked on light
My form to you would change not till I died.
This is the letter that I should not write.

Will my devotion ever suffer blight?
You are so English, passion stultified.
Am I so cloying, clinging, in your sight?

My little dog, Tonton, brings you delight.
I shall bequeath him to you when I've died.
This is the letter that I should not write.
Am I so cloying, clinging, in your sight?

Beryl Cross

A Therapeutic Villanelle

I'm spending too much time on work, I know,
The pressure's putting lines upon my face.
I'd like to sit and watch the flowers grow.

Sometimes I feel the tears begin to flow:
I'm leaden tired, I'm desperate for some space,
I'm spending too much time on work. I know!

Do they want blood? Why don't they bloody go?
I'll crack if I continue at this pace.
I need to sit and watch the flowers grow.

Those piles of paperwork oppress me so,
They never seem to shrink, it's a disgrace.
I'm spending too much time on work, I know.

If I could take my time and take it slow,
If life could be a pleasure, not a race,
Perhaps I'd sit and watch the flowers grow.

If I got bored, there's places I could go,
I'd stretch my limbs, write poetry, find grace.
Must get to spend less time on work - although
I might do more than just watch flowers grow.

Maggie Eisner

A SINGLE ARTIFICIAL ROSE

One single artificial rose
Placed in your hand, impulsively
Love is as far as one heart knows.

Unframed by words, this picture shows
Tentative truths which you may see
A single artificial rose.

Silk petals sleep - they never close
On feelings that must always be
Love is as far as one heart knows.

Places where such a flower grows
Shaded in trembling secrecy
The single artificial rose

Slips through our space - and time it shows
Caught in a glance, one moment free
Love is as far as one heart knows.

Marking my time with constancy
In your small hands, balance the key
My single artificial rose
Love is as far as my heart knows.

John Calvert

NEVER SAID LOVE YOU

Never said love you, now too late,
Your sudden death has left me sad,
Not just my mum, more like a mate.

If I'd only foreseen your fate,
To lose you like that made me bad,
Never said love you, now too late.

Horrid to die on your birth date,
Was close to you, this makes me glad,
Not just my mum, more like a mate.

I tried hard others to placate,
When all I felt was very mad,
Never said love you, now too late.

Will miss seeing you at your gate,
Shared lots of memories you had,
Not just my mum, more like a mate.

Went to various towns of late,
Many places not been with Dad,
Never said love you, now too late,
Not just my mum, more like a mate.

S Mullinger

PANORAMA

Through winding country lane
Between the fields of corn
Drenched, glistening in the rain.

The horses pull and strain
With plough from early morn
Through winding country lane

And do they feel the pain
As they with toil are worn
Drenched, glistening in the rain.

The stable weathervane
Creaks with the hunter's horn
Through winding country lane.

While fox hides in the grain
His heart both rent and torn
Drenched, glistening in the rain.

From hurt, what do we gain?
For we are equal born
Through winding country lane
Drenched, glistening in the rain.

Jill Thompson Barker

VILLANELLE FOR TWO KITTENS: KENT 2000

Bubastis may not claim them yet
Our guests awaited anxiously
Perfect in their majesty as Set

We shall cherish them you bet
May we love them perfectly
Bubastis may not claim them yet

From Ramsgate fair they were 'to let'.
Our homes are shaped for harmony
Perfect in their majesty as Set

Their eyes would turn to our debt
For we must care for them most assiduously
Bubastis may not claim them yet

We have not yet fixed to vet
When we do, it will be anxiously
Perfect in their majesty as Set

They await us, ours to get
We will travel most joyously
Bubastis may not claim them yet
Perfect in their majesty as Set

Joy Sheridan

ON THE EDGE

My mind is like a butterfly
It flits to and fro in my head
Is there no peace, be still I cry.

I set myself a task to try
But seem to lose the path I tread
My mind is like a butterfly.

Patterns appear, I wonder why
My sanity hangs by a thread
Is there no peace, be still I cry.

I look above and search the sky
Engulfed in fear, heart heavy as lead
My mind is like a butterfly.

Feel warm and drowsy, here I lie
Soft voices call, kind words are said
Is there no peace, be still I cry.

My plea is answered, sleep is nigh
I drift and dream, safe in my bed.
My mind is like a butterfly
Is there no peace, be still I cry.

Margaret Wilson

DARK THOUGHTS

Why should my world be cold and black
When life's colour should be white?
Where is the warmth I seem to lack?

I go upstairs and hit the sack
Then lie and think throughout the night,
Why should my world be cold and black?

The tension in my rope is slack.
Why should life be just a fight?
Where is the warmth I seem to lack?

Why should I be on the wrong tack,
The winning post beyond my sight?
Why should my world be cold and black?

Why am I stretched upon life's rack,
Why does my living seem so trite?
Where is the warmth I seem to lack?

Will someone point to the right track,
Show me the way to healing light?
Why should my world be cold and black,
Where is the warmth I seem to lack?

Frank Keetley

INTRANSIENCE

The end is nigh, I'll soon give up the fray.
When thoughts of coffins in my mind unfold
I aim to live for ever and a day.

Construct a pyramid, postpone decay,
When pharaohs say with auspices foretold:
The end is nigh, I'll soon give up the fray.

Or should a dynasty obsess me, say?
By siring sons and heirs in manner bold
I aim to live for ever and a day.

Devise a concept - 'soul' - begin to pray.
No matter if I say when matter's cold,
The end is nigh, I'll soon give up the fray.

We seek intransience in ev'ry way,
What happens next I'd like to have unrolled.
I aim to live for ever and a day.

Impermanence distorts my mortal clay;
You'll know, my verse enduring, when you're told
The end is nigh, I'll soon give up the fray,
I aim to live for ever and a day.

Robert Montgomery

THE OLD CAMPAIGNER

The old campaigner still keeps on the go.
He is as prickly as a roving bramble,
he's difficult but yet we love him so.

He turns up everywhere, is in the know.
He does not hurry as he likes to amble.
The old campaigner still keeps on the go.

His lengthy rhetoric will ebb and flow,
epigrammatic but prefers to ramble.
He's difficult but yet we love him so.

On every march for justice he will show,
in gnomic woolly hat you'll see him shamble.
The old campaigner still keeps on the go.

He's open-hearted, kind to friend and foe
but when his rage may boil is just a gamble.
He's difficult but yet we love him so.

Year in, year out, in sun, in rain, in snow,
it's that old Torriano wimble wamble.
The old campaigner still keeps on the go,
he's difficult but yet we love him so.

Dinah Livingstone

LOVE-GIFT

The wind is sighing in the cypress tree.
No more does joy her gentle beauty show -
You were my music and my poetry.

Now here I wait alone in misery;
You lie so cold beneath the shrouding snow.
The wind is sighing in the cypress tree.

And yet your voice re-echoes still in me,
Though, while you lived, however could I know
You were my music and my poetry?

I did not understand how it could be:
And yet, perhaps you teach me now, although
The wind is sighing in the cypress tree.

For all I held my right, unthinkingly,
Was, truly, sacramental gift - and so,
You were my music and my poetry.

And now, transforming all my agony,
Your gentleness enfolds me as I go.
The wind is sighing in the cypress tree.
You are my music and my poetry.

Jackie Lapidge

THE CONVALESCENT

Shot myself in the foot
Yesterday - or was it today
I put the hole in my boot?

It wasn't astute,
The critics will say,
Shooting myself in the foot.

My wife, for example, cares not a hoot
That friendless I lay
With a hole in my boot;

And who can refute
That I might fade away
Shot by myself in the foot?

Or deny the insurance will seek to dispute
Having to pay
For the hole in my boot?

But - 'C'est la vie', old chap - thanks for the fruit!
Good day, my dear fellow, no need to stay
With old shot in the foot,
Hole in the boot.

Terry Smith

CATS IN THE AIR!

The panda continued to stare,
As pigs flew past the window
Cats are in the air!

The sand in Mogware,
Travelled to where, it could see the water
flow.
The panda continued to stare.

As spiders jumped over the beetle's lair,
Worms crawled past a crow.
Cats are in the air!

Rats and mice come out to play, but careful
of the mayor!
The pea-green boat began to grow,
The panda continued to stare.

Symptoms were aware,
That their human on sugar was low.
Cats are in the air!

Cats and rats, pandas and mice, all riding on
a square
All, a ball could surely throw.
The panda continued to stare.
Cats are in the air!

Claire Field (11)

REMEMBRANCE - VILLAGE GREEN

Before the monument the strangers stand;
The rowan trees in morning's soft breeze sway.
The older woman holds a small boy's hand.

They read the roll - young men who served their land
Went off to war, one dim-remembered day.
Before the monument the strangers stand

Then move a little nearer, nearer and
Caress a name, still clear, upon the clay.
The older woman holds a small boy's hand,

Recalls the halcyon summers - sea, the sand;
One last, lost August, years and years away.
Before the monument, the strangers stand.

Beyond the rowan and the stone, a band
Has gathered - it's the village fete, today.
The older woman holds a small boy's hand,

He is so young. What can he understand
Of ancient pain? This hour is his, for play.
Before the monument, the strangers stand.
The woman, firmly, holds the small boy's hand.

Gwenda M Owen

THE NEW MILLENNIUM . . .

Maybe the world is ready but are we?
The millennium nearing from the corner
Wanting to greet us, think, how will it be?

Will it bring and create new goals, maybe
Keep old ideas wrapped under cover.
Maybe the world is ready, but are we?

Will life on earth improve? Wait and see
This new millennium, around the corner
Wanting to greet us, think how will it be?

Will humanity enjoy peace? Could the
Dreams of happiness be revived, greener.
Maybe the world is ready, but are we?

Lost ideals of long ago discarded, could be
Shading life's borrowed time-burner!
Wanting to greet us, think, how will it be?

Memories once wrapped in gold maybe
Revived, new beginnings all to see
Maybe the world is ready, but are we?
Wanting to greet us, think, how will it be?

Anna Elliott

THE ALMOST TIME

Baby can almost walk.
She can nearly crawl.
She's trying to talk.

Gives us quite a shock,
Thought she was going to fall.
Baby can almost walk.

Dress her in a frilly frock.
Make her look like a doll.
She's trying to talk.

Sometimes solid as a rock,
Then she begins to stall.
Baby can almost walk.

She'll babble around the clock,
Then say nothing at all.
She's trying to talk.

She'll fall and take a knock,
Then get up and stand tall.
Baby can almost walk,
She's trying to talk.

Margaret C Rae

VILLANELLE

Love is at a loose end;
We have lost the plot it's plain to see
And it's no use trying to pretend.

There's no remorse to comprehend;
It's run its course and we both agree,
Love is at a loose end.

We would not achieve a blend;
Our dispute defies a remedy
And it's no use trying to pretend.

Neither or us would bend;
We confess our error honestly,
Love is at a loose end.

We have no dispute to defend;
This is the way it was meant to be
And it's no use trying to pretend.

It's all part of a growing trend -
Our friends have called it a calamity;
Love is at a loose end
And it's no use trying to pretend.

Keith Byam

HONESTLY

When you want something to be true
Listen to voices more keenly,
Then believe the one who tells you

Their fear as your conviction grew,
How you desire so meanly
When you want something to be true.

Protest that you already knew
It hopeless dreaming. Really?
Then believe the one who tells you

Carefully their worry: the hue
Of your thin face, staring palely
When you want something to be true.

The substance and idea of who-
Ever fades eventually.
Then believe the one who tells you.

You ask some strangers for a clue
And wait for what you wish to see
When you want something to be true.
Then believe the one who tells you.

Claire Sheridan

CHRISTINE AT TWENTY-FOUR

Christine at twenty four
Soft August breezes sigh
Behold! Christine no more.

The wedding dress she wore
A shroud in death to lie,
Christine at twenty four.

Sad the swallows dip and soar
And hear the blackbirds cry
Behold! Christine no more.

Ageless now; in my heart's core
I will remember till I die,
Christine at twenty four.

Vanquished all that I adore
I cry to heaven why must I
Behold! Christine no more.

As sorrow fills my every pore
I sob out to the summer sky,
Christine at twenty four
Behold! Christine no more.

Tony Coyle

AWAY FROM ME

I wish you weren't so far away from me,
How much you're missed you'll never really know,
Each time you have to go across the sea.

A sailor's wife is very hard to be,
The nights are lonely and the days pass slow,
I wish you weren't so far away from me.

While other men are home each night for tea,
I sit alone before the firelight's glow,
Each time you have to go across the sea.

It's cold in bed with no one there but me,
I long to hold you close when lights are low,
I wish you weren't so far away from me.

What of shore leave when your time is free?
D'you drink in taverns where the 'night girls' go?
Each time you have to go across the sea.

But do you long for home in bed with me
When buffeted by waves as night winds blow?
I wish you weren't so far away from me,
Each time you have to go across the sea.

Ailsa Keen

My Best Friend

How I miss you Mum now you have gone away.
You meant so much to me when you were here.
I wish you were back home with me to stay.

That smile on your face I miss every day,
God will always look after you my precious dear.
How I miss you Mum now you have gone away.

All I can do is kneel down and pray
And when I am sad I can feel a tear.
I wish you were back home with me to stay.

I remember all the things that you used to say.
I always felt close to you when you were near.
How I miss you Mum now you have gone away.

I hope you are at rest now Mum where you lay.
You told me not to worry and enjoy every year.
I wish you were back home with me to stay.

We spent many hours together when we used to play.
And always gave into me, for me to have my way.
How I miss you Mum now you have gone away.
I wish you were back home with me to stay.

Colin H Cross

TIMEKEEPER

I sit upon the mantlepiece
In a house that's growing old
What I do will never cease
I have a face of brass so bold.

I have friends that rest upon your wrist
Some of my family live in towers
I have a key that you must twist
So I can count away the hours.

With my hands I show the time
I point at numbers so you can see
On the hour I will chime
A timekeeper that is me.

Tick, tick, tick, tock
I'm just your normal household clock.

A F Mace

TEMPTATION

Oscar Wilde told the world he could resist,
Could shun, anything except temptation.
Sweet, indeed are fruits that are forbidden
And thrilling, chilling is the stolen kiss.
Exciting urgent, whispered promises,
Touch and taste, to feel the exultation
Knowing many man-made laws are broken,
What satisfaction ever exceeds this?
Tomorrow, maybe, is the time to pay,
Will the high expense alloy the pleasure?
Here are the scales, take them and will you weigh
The cost against many things I treasure?
And when my secrets all have been betrayed
How many hearts are broken, lives destroyed?

Hazel Wellings

MAKING OUR MARK

Hoping to make a mark upon our time
That, leaving, they shall not have lived in vain
Some paint, some sing, and some express in rhyme
A wisp of beauty touched, to find again.

But modern thinkers lately turn away
From loveliness, to settle on things new
And strange. They celebrate death and decay,
Paying their homage with a jaundiced view.

A fresh approach to culture has been found
Where standards bow before the latest craze:
Youth strives to shock and twist, to search around
Beyond, beneath the glory of our days.

But we, being closer to our gruesome end
Cling to true beauty as a precious friend.

Sylvia Tyers

THE POET'S REMORSE

When inspiration has flown far away
Poets start feeling a deep remorse,
But look around and don't feel grey
Marvellous colours surround us with force.

Each wonderful season that upon us dawns
Brings fresh ideas to urgently express,
Words of wisdom - words of warmth
Verses tinged with sadness, and with happiness.

There is time for some reflection
Look back to your childhood dreams,
Shelve all those slips of bitter rejection
And get moving on positive schemes.

Knuckle down, work hard each day
Success is bound to come your way.

Val Bermingham

UNFOUNDED HOPE

With winter gone, now greet the spring.
The flowers open, showing as they do
The coloured petals, stamens gold and true.
And perfume scents the air as blossoms swing
While birds on branches, just as sweetly, sing.
All promise is of the coming life anew
As birds build nests and bees are active through
A world so honied, all sweetness, everything.

But spring, so full of promise soon will die
The flowers fade and drop, their purpose done,
Each petal dropping gentler than a sigh
As summer brings its heat, its murd'rous sun.
Then autumn follows, winds and frost that vie
To destroy ling'ring life and leave us none.

Ann Harrison

LOVE'S MUSIC

We first met whilst at university
Our looks across each other through the glass
Were like a prelude at a master class
And we the faithful students in the library.
Next came the fugue - a mix of friends and fears;
Each one of us was spoken for, but yet
There was a part of both of us was set
For more, and ready to risk hurt and tears:

And so it came about we met once more
Through mutual friends, who'd heard the songs we hummed
In harmony and helped us write the score,
By reuniting us where we were numbed
By pride, false notes and yet still looking for
Each other in a book of melodies well thumbed.

Mark Lello

REGRET

What of your life you'd rather I'd ignored?
The silent look, the oft neglected need?
Your broken word so often I deplored?
Repeated pleas that you would never heed?

The many nights you came home very late,
Leaving me alone and sitting up?
Your willing readiness to break a date
And offer me a bitter-tasting cup?

And yet I know that I'm imperfect too,
I had my failings and must share the blame.
My lack of thought, and hurt I brought to you,
Cause me to hang my saddened head in shame.

I only know that now you're not with me,
I would that I once more your face might see.

R A S

THE DANCE OF DEATH

Do we fill our lives with important things
With study and with pleasure hours,
Enjoy the summer and the spring
Take time for nature, and her flowers?

Or, waste we time, acquire and save
Make no attempt, to find a friend
Are we too eager to turn the page
Wrapped up in self and . . . I pretend?

Dull humour driving us, I fear . . .
In realms of seething discontent.
Although the purpose may seem clear
We're blind to what it really meant.

Each movement, step . . . and every breath
A pattern in the dance of death.

Brenda Robson-Eifler

RAILWAY JOURNEY

Alone, funeral-bound, I read and doze.
The sun, forlornly shining through the mist,
Casts wintry rays on distant bare hedgerows
And frosty fields by its wan beams are kissed.
Pathetic fallacy - to think the year,
Near-ending, shares Love's pain or this goodbye
To part of my existence, things held dear.
(There's more than one life lost when good friends die.)

I wake and lurch along the hurtling train,
See you, my late Love, in the buffet car.
Our idyll's over; it won't live again.
How strange that one so near should be so far!

Though cold your proffered hand, Time makes amends.
Surely I'll find a new Love, keep old friends . . .

Jacqueline Abendstern

SAY, BELOVED, SHALL WE MEET?

Say, beloved, shall we meet
outside the dark wood's gate at dawn,
and seek at last a safe retreat?

We'll head along Great Rafton Street,
and glimpse the sea before the morn.
Say, beloved, shall we meet?

And dearest we'll the wild birds greet,
and joyful pass through fields of corn,
and seek at last a safe retreat,

and soon we'll spy the white ships' fleet
prepared before the day was born.
Say, beloved, shall we meet?

And long before the day's noon-heat
we'll sail beyond the reach of scorn,
and seek at last a safe retreat.

In a good ship's prow we'll take our seat,
and laugh to be the wild wind's pawn.
Say, beloved, shall we meet,
and seek at last a safe retreat?

Jennifer Hashmi

A SONNET TO WINTER

Dawn's eerie shadows, - mystic and ethereal,
Barren bark of trees - dressed - all - over white,
Children gaze agog, at the eerie scene . . .
Then shout with joy - 'I spy with my little eye!'

Snow-laden branches, creak, bend and sway,
'Moel Famau Mount', a giant clad in white,
A magic moment of rare experience . . .
Time, for fairy-tale Pantomime on ice.

Snow laden branches, creak, bend and sway,
Moel Framau mount, 'Tall Giant' clad in white,
Fairy tales, pantomime of skating mice
Like frail gossamer, will fade away in time!

Hold fast your fairy tales of make believe,
Apparitions will soon disperse from scene,
Long, dark, foreboding barren days we'll see,
Before the rising sap, gives life to trees.

Nature in her various aspect - stagnant,
Till ignited, by the glow of springtime.

Marion de Bruyn

LEAD THE WAY

If I could only get up to my feet
and walk about whenever I did please,
I'd be just like the others in the street
the image of it only serves to tease.

If I felt well then I would take my chance
and gad about wherever I did choose,
perhaps I'd hike or maybe I'd just dance
whichever one I'd need a pair of shoes.

If I was better, I'd grab at your hand
and careful not to stand upon your toes,
the crowd would clap; I'd signal to the band
to play our chosen song 'La vie en rosé'.

Together we would whirl around the stage
an excerpt from a lovely printed page.

Michelle Broadbent

OUCH, I HAVE HIT MY THUMB!

Ouch, I have hit my thumb!
It is slowly turning blue.
How could I be so dumb!

It is alright for some
Who carpenter's skills pursue.
Ouch, I have hit my thumb!

It starts to feel quite numb,
And my lack of skill I rue.
How could I be so dumb!

It's swelling, throb, throb, thrum,
As it goes a deeper hue.
Ouch, I have hit my thumb!

I grit my teeth and hum,
I will not weep, boo-hoo-hoo.
How could I be so dumb!

Bandage it, so cumbersome.
I can work no more, it's true.
Ouch, I have hit my thumb!
How could I be so dumb!

Catherine Hartland

No Moon, No Stars . . .

No moon, no stars are out tonight,
The air so still and cold.
All people now are gone from sight.

The empty sky, its endless height
Brings out the need to hold.
No moon, no stars are out tonight.

Alone in this, my throat feels tight,
No child here to enfold.
All people now are gone from sight.

Without the one who kept me bright,
Who brought that spark of gold,
No moon, no stars are out tonight.

The rage inside, a need to fight
That surging rush of old.
All people now are gone from sight.

Like darkness without candlelight
This grief, as yet untold.
No moon, no stars are out tonight,
All people now are gone from sight.

Rosemary Bowman

THE APPLE TREE

Winter is here, there's ice and snow,
Alas, no leaves on my apple tree,
But spring is coming, this I know.

Strong and cruel the wind does blow
And weak the sun, because you see,
Winter is here, there's ice and snow.

The ice-bound streams will cease to flow,
Birds to warmer climes do flee,
But spring is coming, this I know.

My tree will blossom in spring although
Now it is cold, for you must agree,
Winter is here, there's ice and snow.

Rosy apples with cheeks aglow
In autumn my tree did give to me,
But spring is coming, this I know.

Frost-laden branches drooping low,
Oh apple tree, listen to me.
Winter is here, there's ice and snow,
But Spring is coming, this I know.

Doris Dowling

A SIGH FOR LOVE

My life is like a winter's day.
My love has gone, I know not why.
I begged him but he would not stay.

No more to see those eyes of gray
My love has gone, I can but sigh.
My life is like a winter's day.

Why must he leave and go his way,
I'll not forget him though I try.
I begged him but he would not stay.

Cold was my bed as down I lay,
Where he spoke of love but he did lie.
My life is like a winter's day.

Down on my knees I fell to pray.
He did not heed my tortured cry.
I begged him but he would not stay.

Why did my lover need to stray,
Leaving my heart to shrink and die
My life is like a winter's day.
I begged him but he would not stay.

Nell Arch

UFO Man

UFO Man what do you think I
am?
running round the earth
a short life after birth,
have our brains enough room
if we need to cram?

You often see a funny man
telling you he's Uncle Sam,
when I laugh what do you think
of mirth?
UFO Man what do you think I
am?

Have you noticed how far we have
come since the old tram?
Do you care about girth?
Have our brains enough room
if we need to cram?

Did you ever try our drinks
even a little dram?
To you have I much worth?
UFO Man what do you think I
am?

I suppose you have your own
form of Adam,
or, do you only like the earth?
Have our brains enough room
if we need to cram?

To you our brains must hardly
weigh a gram,
have you just found us intellects
of dearth?
UFO Man what do you think I am?
Have our brains enough room if
we need to cram?

Jean Paisley

I STOOD ALONE

I stood alone beside the sea,
The sunlight glistened all around,
I heard his voice, he spoke to me.

From every doubt he made me free,
He set my feet on solid ground,
I stood alone beside the sea.

His love is with me constantly;
In stillness and without a sound
I heard his voice, he spoke to me.

With heart and mind in harmony
His peace and joy that day I found;
I stood alone beside the sea.

I followed him, he holds the key,
I laid my fears and mistrust down,
I heard his voice, he spoke to me.

I went to him on bended knee,
My true identity unbound
I stood alone beside the sea,
I heard his voice, he spoke to me.

Valerie Sutton

MY HEART

My heart is full of fire
My love is just for you
You are my heart's desire
    To deny my feelings, I would be a liar
    My heart is just so true
    My heart is full of fire
I hope your love for me, will never ever tire
It hurts to love like lovers do
You are my heart's desire
    Your beauty and your grace, I also admire
    Also kindness and generosity anew
    My heart is full of fire
If we ever parted, to me it would be dire
I love you so much, it hurts so true
You are my heart's desire
    So let's let our hearts conspire
    To be as one forever, not two
    My heart is full of fire
    You are my heart's desire.

C S Fricker

THE LOST BOYS
(Dedicated to Rory and Oscar)

Your Daddy loved you boys -
More than you will ever know;
You were his treasures, his pride, his joys.

At work amid the grease and noise,
He toiled through years in sun and snow,
Your Daddy loved you, boys.

At home, at play, all hoi pollois;
In his laughter, his eyes would show -
You were his treasures, his pride, his joys.

In spirit he's with you and still enjoys -
Your triumphs, successes (and your woe)
Your Daddy loved, you boys.

Although the gap he left still cloys -
He, from the skies, looks down below,
You were his treasures, his pride, his joys.

Yet, through your lives, he still employs
The love and warmth he once could show.
Your daddy loved you boys -
You were his treasures, his pride, his joys.

Nettie Killen

EDGE OF FANTASY

Watching the darkness come for me,
I raise my fists, prepared to fight,
Living on the edge of fantasy.

How foolish - stupid - can I be?
I know now, this idea wasn't right!
Watching the darkness come for me . . .

Closing my eyes I refused to see,
A horrid face coming from the night . . .
Living on the edge of fantasy.

But then a surge, I felt so free,
So I turned (and stood) to face the sight,
Watching the darkness come for me.

Would I be strong enough to be,
The victor against this great dark might?
Living on the edge of fantasy.

And yet I knew I had my destiny,
And filled in strength from some unknown light,
Watching the darkness come for me:
Living on the edge of fantasy.

Tobias Nicholls

LOST LOVE

My love is lost to me she's found someone new
Being without her is breaking my heart
Oh how I wish I was still with you.

The day she left is a day I shall forever rue
Such sorrow is tearing me apart
My love is lost to me she's found someone new.

I hoped she would return to me, alas it was not true
It grieves me that we had to part
Oh how I wish I was still with you.

Life is passing me by I feel so blue
To me you are a work of art
My love is lost to me she's found someone new.

Happiness in life I must be due
My search for love anew must start
Oh how I wish I was still with you.

I realise now that we are through
Our time together will remain forever in my heart
My love is lost to me she's found someone new
Oh how I wish I was still with you.

K J Wood

JUST SAYING

Man will wait for both time and tide
And why should milk he spill.
In the sun you tan your hide
When you've time to kill.

If clothes make the man
Be a friend indeed.
Who had clothes when time began
Go out and have a feed.

Never walk under a ladder
That is for just faint hearted.
Never sleep with a full bladder
A fool and his money parted.

Look a gift horse in the mouth
Open up your north and south.

Colin Allsop

TO BESS OUR RESCUED BITCH

My heart is broke for you, my Bess, for naught
Can heal the loss of kind and grateful eyes;
Unblinking, wise in gaze at me, with tries
To catch my eye for praise of you, or aught
That signalled bonds that you to me had wrought.
We rescued you from chains and silent cries,
For cruel men had nearly closed your eyes
In early death. But us you'd always sought:
A family; just ideal, and made for you,
With love and decent grub, and warmth and bed
Your own, and not cold concrete; near to death,
As painful pups, for greed, became too few.
Then lies were cooked of bites. You looked unfed.
You fought, but failing heart slow stilled your breath.

Epilogue

But now, in our old wood, you rest in earth;
A magic rowan tree now guards your worth.

Brian MacDonald

PLAY THE GAME

Just toe the line and play the game
ever on in all you do,
'tho nothing ever stays the same.

It's often hard to take the blame,
to shoulder what life throws at you,
- just toe the line and play the game.

Don't e'er look back the way you came,
enjoy the now, the present view,
'tho nothing ever stays the same.

It isn't wrong to hope for fame
but if the honours don't accrue
just toe the line and play the game.

Face the challenge, fight the shame
content with what life leads you to,
'tho nothing ever stays the same.

And when, remembering, they say your name
they'll say that what you said was true
just toe the line and play the game
. . . 'tho nothing ever stays the same.

Brenda Heath

OUR LOVE

You mean all the world to me
I cannot tell a lie
Our love was meant to be.

Oh my darling can't you see
For you I would die
You mean all the world to me.

You're in my mind constantly
And my heart soars high
Our love was meant to be

My dreams are filled with so much glee
So never say goodbye
You mean all the world to me.

I'll never love another such as thee
On the wings of love I fly
Our love was meant to be.

Your arms enfold me like the branches of a tree
I look up at you and let out a sigh
You mean all the world to me
Our love was meant to be.

Sheila A Dinsdale

THE GORSE IS NEVER OUT OF BLOOM

Amid the musky blossom of the gorse
We found a long deserted railway track.
I shall recall with no thought of remorse

The golden days we spent on foot and horse
With compass, map, and well-filled haversack
Amid the musky blossom of the gorse,

Tracing the stream to find its bubbling source,
Alone with kingfisher and stickleback.
I shall recall with no thought of remorse

The joy of nature's primal driving force
That fuelled our youthful passions cardiac
Amid the musky blossom of the gorse.

The scented blooms that each month reinforce
The memories of all that now I lack
I shall recall with no thought of remorse.

Nostalgia in old age will but endorse
The time worn dreams that take me gladly back
Amid the musky blossom of the gorse
I shall recall with no thought of remorse.

Grahame Godsmark

JOSHUA

With innocence and wisdom there
He looks up at his world with sparkling blue
And a love close nestled, now laid bare

He challenges with brazen stare
His tempers are a sight to view
With innocence and wisdom there

His words are few, yet spoke with care
Midst a laugh that grabs the heart from you
And a love close nestled, now laid bare

He often cuddles and kisses with flare
With joyful triumph he learns what's true
With innocence and wisdom there

He toddles and topples, I know not where
Is independent and helpless too
And a love close nestled, now laid bare

So turn away now, if you dare
For those of his calibre are very few
With innocence and wisdom there
And a love close nestled, now laid bare.

Tricia Cuming

GOD'S AMAZING WORLD

As adopted families of God's amazing world
We are legally appointed by divine grace,
To strive; as disciplined human race.
Richly nourished, by the living word
Retrospective of the two-edged sword
That guides us into picturesque place;
As the world is built superbly, on divine base
And the half has never been told.

God's amazing world is perfectly made.
Ideally designed and furnished in every way,
With all foundations uniquely laid;
And shall neither shrink, nor decay -
Nor will; the amazing beauty fade
Throughout earth's glorified eternal day.

E Coke

LATE LOVE FLOWERING

If you should seek some comfort from me now
in words I have no aptitude to use,
and question in your deepest thoughts just how
my cruel silence labours to confuse.
Then should I say, with all my humbleness,
such words were never easy on my tongue
from early days I knew no gentleness
to fill my hours with love when I was young.
And so it is, at time of evening's fade,
when tiredness makes other men feel old,
still here I linger sadly in the shade
that blights my senses with its barren cold.
I want to turn back time and gently make
of words a coloured garland you can take.

It is too late to light within a fire
to warm a closed and dumbly aching heart,
to find the love that ever will inspire
unbidden words to speak when we must part.
Does urgent love depart when we grow old,
desire quickly burn to ember glow?
Or can we come in from the biting cold
to peace and warmth that never did we know.
If you will smile at me with lips and eyes
and catch me with its wistful loving gleam,
could I escape from being ever wise,
return to dwell within some youthful dream.
Love's fashion is a quick and trifling spell
that weaves a captive web to bind us well.

Ann Rutherford

GHOST

I am the ghost, within the body that you see.
Forever ailing, awaiting release of the pain I feel every day.
If only I could from my Earthly bodily anchor flee.
No more hurt or penance for my life to pay.

I am a soul within awaiting freedom come.
Longing for Heaven's welcome reach and touch.
My flesh is frail, nay weak, my blood is done.
Is asking time to quickly pass a request too much.

Once I was a star always young and shining bright
Sparkling like a diamond reaching high towards the sky.
Always my life ahead with love and happiness in sight
Now my body fades, become pale waiting to die

I say farewell to family and friends I leave behind
I meet my maker and make amends, pain denied, peace I find.

Harry Eastwood

UNTITLED

Romance, I know, is Nature's mating game
And base biology its driving force
And chemistry, not love, dictates the course
Of rituals illumined by passion's flame;
Keen yearning fit the tender soul to maim
Mute language of the gene is but its source
To salve its pain I have but one recourse:
Capitulate to Nature in thy name;
And though romance is merely Nature's ploy
For propagation of the human race,
And carnal instinct with the pschye vies,
Congenital in every girl and boy;
Resides more beauty in thy form, and grace
Than would redeem all Nature's cunning lies.

N G Charnley

NIGHT WALK SONNET

The warm spring air has turned to cooler eve;
Beneath the cloudless sky the night is stilled.
Cold air bites sharp, my stinging skin to cleave,
My staring eyes with pin-pricked stars are filled.
The lone fox hoarsely to the vixen barks,
Aroused, she answers his alluring call.
A restless dog on howling match embarks
And ewes protect their lambs behind the wall,
While hedgerow creatures tremble at the tune;
But my dog's feet go tripping down the lane.
Above, the cratered face of silver moon
A night-watch will upon the world maintain
And there, in arching, royal blue dome on high,
Cassiopeia writes across the sky.

Sheila E Harvey

RICHARD

Believe in those dear charms
Window on the world framed
Better the evil you invite
Leave the room feel blamed

Gentle pushing forward the system
Back harder here or there forever
As from now say his one
Is new fresh from wherever

Submit the letter read aloud
Richard, Richard, Richard, Richard
A free man no longer bowed
Down with burdens or such like

A day for every soul
Flowers in the crystal bowl

S M Thompson

TOGETHER WE WILL BRAVE THE WORLD

Together we will brave the world,
When others criticise and shout;
Our fingers linked, both hearts unfurled.

Your hair around my shoulders curled;
Our steadfast friendship keeps them out,
Together we will brave the world.

Challenges are weapons hurled
To thrust comradeship into doubt:
Our fingers linked, both hearts unfurled.

Your dancing eyes, full skirts that twirled,
Those rosebud lips that smile and pout:
Together we will brave the world.

Rainbows and roses dewdrop pearled,
Treasured, fine, not to be without:
Our fingers linked both hearts unfurled.

Stave off the insults round us whirled:
This love we cannot be without.
Together we will brave the world,
Our fingers linked, both hearts unfurled.

Andy Bryan

MY LOVE

My love, I knew so long ago,
Where are you now?
You were Heaven sent to me.

I miss you so,
Where did you go?
My Love, I knew so long ago.

Where are you now?
First Love of mine?
You were Heaven sent to me.

I search and search,
Anywhere, every place, every face,
My Love, I knew so long ago.

I was such a fool to let you go,
Time has not changed how I feel,
You were Heaven sent to me.

And every day, I pray,
Our paths will meet again,
My Love, I knew so long ago,
You were Heaven sent to me.

Susan Brown

HEAR MY PRAYER

Dear Lord in Heaven, hear my prayer,
And wipe away my tears of shame -
Forgive my Lord, I know you're there!

With eyes wide open, and aware -
I sinned against your holy name . . .
Dear Lord in Heaven, hear my prayer!

Console me with your loving care -
Absolve me from all mortal blame . . .
Forgive me Lord, I know you're there!

One moment in one brief affair -
Now life will never be the same . . .
Dear Lord in Heaven, hear my prayer!

I feel your presence everywhere -
You mingle with my tears of shame . . .
Forgive me Lord, I know you're there!

Is my soul beyond repair?
Must I perish in the flame?
Dear Lord in Heaven, hear my prayer . . .
Forgive me Lord, I know you're there!

Russell Humphrey

RED RUNNING ROOSTER

Little Red Rooster is miles ahead now
He has got to win the race
I can see him in my dreams

He's a flash of chestnut red
A dazzling creature that never loses pace
Little Red Rooster is miles ahead now

Over barriers, through fields of obstacles
He flies so high, so full of grace
I can see him in my dreams

The colour of my life, soars the skies
I pray hurry now, make haste
Little Red Rooster is miles ahead now

Our adrenaline pumps, wild and free
Another fence coming that we must face
I can see him in my dreams

Red, so lithe and full of vibrance
As we hurdle through infinite space
Little Red Rooster is miles ahead now
I can see him in my dreams.

Miriam Eissa

THE BOA CONSTRICTOR

With eyes as black as mould
His skin the finest of leather
Through the night he strolled
Desirous he coaxed and cajoled
Hunting his prey in elements weather
With eyes black as mould
Stalking the territory he controlled
Searching between the thickest heather
Through the night he strolled
Slithering jungle floor he patrolled
Armoured scales deceitfully cleaver
With eyes as black as mould
A deadly serpent mighty and bold
Worms his way light as a feather
Through the night he strolled
Constricting his prey with powerful hold
Gaping jaws grab and tightly tether
With eyes as black as mould
Through the night he strolled

Ann Hathaway

LOVE STORY

It is with joy I think of you
And all the things you meant to me:
My memories stay, forever new.

I wonder if you miss me too,
Recalling how it used to be?
It is with joy I think of you.

My heart still aches. What can I do?
Though I've tried hard to set you free,
My memories stay, forever new.

Your love for me was strong and true:
It cannot die, I have the key.
It is with joy I think of you.

We dare not meet; I've thought this through.
Somehow I have to make you see
My memories stay, forever new.

And when in heav'n we meet, we two,
We'll live once more in ecstasy.
It is with joy I think of you,
My memories stay, forever new.

Phyllis Spooner

A Sonnet To Life

Oh life! You days of endless toil and strife
A world where earthquake rage and life destroy
Withdraw from my poor heart that wounding knife
Return to days of peace, infectious joy.
No push and shove, no litter on the shore
A frog is croaking, birds are singing sweet
Pain of suffering, aching heart no more
Nature, harmony make my life complete.
A singing stream, a field of green and gold
A sky where sunshine warms and brings a smile
An ideal place where tales of love are told
Escape the raging driver for a while.
Oh life! You days of love and summer sun
Where pain is banned replace with joy and fun.

David Arran

THE BEE

In Ericas and roses and sweet musk,
In fragrant honeysuckle I delight;
I haunt the blooms until the gloom of dusk
Gives churlish way to the descending night.

Oh, lavender and lilac fill my day,
The scent of roses brings me on the breeze
Of summer's joyful dance amidst the hay,
And autumn's playful game among the trees.

The sun lights up my velvet black and gold,
And softly strokes my incandescent wings;
I see the summer's lazy days unfold,
While I am busy with a myriad things.

So through the hazy days 'til; autumn's birth,
To shorter days not filled so much with scent:-
'Til all around this cooling, wintry earth,
There is no sign where all the flowers went.

And as the winter now begins to fall,
There is no sign of me, of me, at all.

Anne Rolfe-Brooker

WHY?

Down in the deep, dark depths of my own mind,
All alone in the world, I now do stand.
My own dear love has left me, gone to rest,
This is not, the retirement we had planned.
What sin did we commit, so bad, so vile,
That nine years on, my grief is still inside?
She left me, though she wished to stay awhile,
But now her strength had gone and so she died.

And though, part of me too, did also fade,
I battled on through life and cast my mark,
With poems, music, humour, friendships made,
Thus letting sunshine in, where there was dark,
Yet thro' these years, in any kind of season,
I still can't see the sense, find the reason.

Peter J Sutton

THE STORM

Looking up into skies full of black clouds,
Knowing that rain will fall in great force,
Static thickening the air stale and coarse,
Thunder rumbling over the great distant grounds,

Lightning crackling like sparks of pain,
Flashing like flickers of bright, light in fear,
Promising to clear the thick atmosphere,
Drawing nearer the storm brings lashing rain,

Washing the earth of its filth and despair,
Working together like a well chosen team,
Thunder, lightning and rain clear the air,
Now the earth has been rinsed until very clean.

It had arrived almost without expectance,
The storm now fades back into non-existence.

Joanne Holmes

SONNET FOR A WEDDING

We are not bound together by the law
Nor by gold rings or vows that we have made
But by the hopefulness of our two hearts
That see into the future unafraid.
Today we join the choir where families sing
As tunefully as any nightingale
When on a summer's evening from dark trees
A song pours out whose beauty cannot stale.
It tells of peaceful times that are to come
As in bad weather we are armed for pain
By sheltering love, so that we surely need
No laws to keep us from the driving rain.
Our names are written in the book of life,
A faithful husband and a loving wife.

Deirdre Armes Smith

SPIRITUAL BLINDNESS

A painful dislocation has occurred,
The people and the Church are 'out of synch'.
The people, plainly, think it is absurd
That clergy will not change the way they think!
The faithful ebb towards sorrow and despair,
Vacate the aisles and vanish from the pew.
Yet, clergymen seem blithely unaware
Parishioners are drifting from their view!
If, sometimes, churches gain, the bishops swear
To congregations up and down the land
That, 'All is well! While ministers are there
What need of change?' They fail to understand
How perilously close the shoals; sad graves
For those who won't discern the tide from waves.

John M Beazley

THE GRAVEYARD

Around the steeple ancient gargoyles grimacing, protrude from stone,
eye drawn to memorial angels, whose silent trumpets call.
Over the churchyard where coloured lichens, many centuries grown.

Voices sing the shepherd psalm in harmonious tone,
echoing in seclusion sweetness, on deaf ears fall.
Around the steeple ancient gargoyles grimacing, protrude from stone.

Brothers and sisters listen here, to Sunday sermons drone
kinsmen through centuries, blessed inside these holy walls.
Over the churchyard where coloured lichens, many centuries grown.

Heart of the village, haven of souls spiritually prone,
discussions by the diocese, held in hallowed halls.
Around the steeple ancient gargoyles grimacing, protrude from stone.

Epitaphs wind and rain erode, gravestones topple down
concealed deep in ivy leaf, composts rotting pall.
Over the churchyard where coloured lichens, many centuries grown.

Wildlife lives in this Eden's green and slow decaying stones,
magically midst tree and herb nature's yearly renewal,
around the steeple ancient gargoyles grimacing, protrude from stone,
over the churchyard where coloured lichens, many centuries grown.

Evelyn Poppy Sawyer

PETE GOSS'S VISION

The twinkle in this sailor's eye
Laying dormant now begins to rise
To meet the challenge, do or die.

Its gleam sweeps masts that reach the sky
To pierce the stars and with them lies
The twinkle in this sailor's eye.

Now his optimism's high
That he can win the biggest prize
To meet the challenge, do or die.

So all his thoughts begin to fly,
Strange forms reflect yet don't disguise
The twinkle in this sailor's eye.

He works so hard to justify
His faith in this great enterprise
To meet the challenge, do or die.

This catamaran will seek to try
Forever to immortalise
The twinkle in this sailor's eye
To meet the challenge, do or die.

Paddy Jupp

THE CHILDREN'S GARDEN PARTY

Shouts of enjoyment rang out through the air,
Active partakers were on every hand,
Laughter and happiness were everywhere.

Children were playing - the dark and the fair
Rushing around all in a happy band.
Shouts of enjoyment rang out through the air.

The sun shone down on the lively scene there,
Flushed faces all by the gentle breeze fanned.
Laughter and happiness were everywhere.

Grown-ups were watching them, without a care
Skipping, the most cheerful girls in the land.
Sounds of enjoyment rang out through the air.

Party food disappeared, tables were bare.
Next, to the sand pit to play in the sand.
Laughter and happiness were everywhere.

Then to the show with the young dancing bear
And the magician - it all went as planned.
Shouts of enjoyment rang out through the air,
Laughter and happiness were everywhere.

Joyce M Turner

A THROW AWAY WORLD

It seems to be a throw away world today,
When at the dump it gives me the hump,
Too much easy money, too much high pay.

No matter what anyone has to say,
They would be told to go and jump,
It seems to be a throw away world today.

On the dump, the weather was bright and gay,
I spotted a bicycle, complete with the pump,
It seems to be a throw away world today.

Then I looked into another large bay,
New things too good for the rubbish dump,
It seems to be a throw away world today.

I cannot see why they are thrown away,
Toys and dolls, some jigsaws all in a clump,
Too much easy money, too much high pay.

They will surely regret it some later day,
Coming down to earth, with a mighty bump.
It seems to be a throw away world today,
Too much easy money, too much high pay.

Frank E Trickett

POETRY, EMANCIPATE ME!

He has no feelings, just words to express
Your inadequate stuttered stumble for purity;
The need to emancipate your cold duress:

'Some wear their silences as more than dress'.
Personified poem doesn't care about me:
He has no feelings, just words to express.

He can drive to the core of: My life's a mess!
Smile contemptuously at your lost dignity,
The need to emancipate your cold duress

With poems, unless
It seeps through forcing equanimity.
He has no feelings, just words to express

The burning anxiety of loneliness.
Oh poetry! You are perfect therapy,
The need to emancipate your cold duress

And fill the hollow emptiness
With intricately rhymed poetry.
He has no feelings, just words to express
The need to emancipate your cold duress.

Sophie Mullins

ANNOUNCED LOVE

For the one love song I want to sing
your love provides my melody
of feelings only you can bring.

A woman, kind and so forgiving,
my inspiration you'll always be
for the one love song I want to sing.

Your love is such a special thing:
my joy is there for all to see
of feelings only you can bring.

With all your heart you keep me going,
your kindly ways have been the key,
for the one love song I want to sing.

Sheltered 'neath your caring wing,
never ever set me free
of feelings only you can bring.

From fading light to early morning,
you gave so much of yourself to me
for the one love song I want to sing,
of feelings only you can bring.

Brian Taylor

ONCE BITTEN

Just to see them smooching, for all to see,
Makes me squirm. It surely cannot last.
You won't catch me, you tell yourself, that's passed.
Been there, done that. I want to be free
From all that turmoil. It's not good for me.
All at sea in the love-boat, tides change fast.
Overboard you're hooked, when the fly is cast.
Then you're landed. Gutted, on your own, lonely.
Out of the blue, you're struck right to the heart,
From a fine feathered arrow, piercing hard.
Nature playing Cupid, striking with its dart,
Quite bowls you over, when you're off your guard.
Stabbed and hooked with love, burning from the start,
Play to win or dodge it. There's no holds barred.

Pauline Boncey

PRESS FORWARD!

It was a cold, disheartening afternoon,
The Lower Fours were waiting for their class.
I left the staff room, not a bit too soon.
'Please let's do something happy, Mrs Bass!'
The Anchor Challenge lay upon a table
And Wordsworth's lines gave me some inspiration.
And so I wondered if they would be able
To compose sonnets for this competition.
We studied scansion, pentameters and stress
And recognised iambic feet, weak, strong.
We counted syllables and, more or less,
Composed some practice verses fourteen lines long.
The girls are only thirteen years of age,
How marvellous if their sonnets reach your page.

Barbara Bass

BOYS?

Boys 4 girls, do they like us or don't they?
Why, if they like us do they start teasing us?
When will they realise, we don't see teasing as play,
And then they wonder why we make such a fuss.

Boys don't understand the concept of secret, silent love;
An accidental brush against the skin in an unconcerning style.
A silent whisper like the singing of a peaceful dove,
A quiet, secret wink, a small, comforting smile.

Instead, when they see us, they turn and run,
We're easy to talk to if they just relax.
How can we like them and think they're fun,
When we only meet them with the writing in a fax.

So if they act like hounds and don't come around,
They'll be looking for love already found.

Cassandra Halliburton (13)

Summer Memories

I look out my window, here's what I see:
The red sun sets behind dark bushy trees,
Beautiful flowers of every colour blossoming with glee,
The blades of grass sway in the evening breeze,
The pond which is home to every type of fish,
The sand box in which I liked to make castles,
The bird house with the bread tray and water dish
And in the shed where my dog leaves his parcels!
The greenhouse full of insects and busy flies,
These will not be here again tomorrow,
All this will change in autumn and then it dies,
The flowers and bees, birds and trees will all go
And I shall be left on my own again,
To endure the cold, misty winter's pain.

Natasha Dogra

29TH FEBRUARY

The time for women of 'modern today'
Is the twenty ninth of February
On this day a young lady may
Ask her love if it's she he will marry

I disagree with this approach to love
What happened to the exercise of rights -
Once every four years is never enough
The men folk should be the ones in these plights

If girls were the ones who knelt on one knee
And a man was the one she proposed to
The girl was who asks 'Will you marry me?'
And he says 'Yes,' and must swear to be true

Then this day would come and men would gain from it
And it would be a boy who wrote this sonnet.

Rickie-Leanne Jackson (13)

FEBRUARY 29TH

I do not see why it should have to be
today and not a single other day
a woman came and asked to marry me,
but if I say 'No!' then I'll have to pay
with silk or even one whole thousand pounds!
I opened my mouth, but no sound came out,
she seemed to think that no way had she found
the man of her dreams 'cause she was about
to go off and leave me in the long grass.
So, I just had to say something quickly.
She looked at me faintly. I said, 'Don't pass out,
I will if you want me to desp'rately.'
She looked at me again and gave a smile.
And guess what? I was smiling back meanwhile.

Victoria Alexander-Wilkins (12)

SONNETS

A sonnet is impossible to write,
I want to give up on this one right now.
I would prefer a chocolate cake to bite,
I want to know just how, oh how, oh how,
How shall I finish this sonnet on time?
I really hate being put on the spot,
I really want to get something to rhyme.
I need a sonnet with a quite good plot,
'Cos this one is absolutely rubbish.
I so much hate writing boring sonnets.
It would be better made up by a fish,
I really now need to give up on it.
If I could, to bed I would go and snooze,
I think this competition I will lose.

Catherine Chuter (13)

SONNET: GHASTLY GYMNASTICS

What is the point of doing gym at school?
As a dangerous sport we could break arms!
Do the teachers like to make us look fools?
Without gym school would be a haven of calm.
Nobody likes to climb ropes like little monkeys,
Or tumble across crash mats on the floor.
Even if the exercise makes muscles chunky,
Gym should be cancelled, I'll do it no more.
Who wants to do box splits on a mat?
When will the teachers start to understand?
Why can't everyone just stay weak and fat
And get rid of gym throughout all the land.
Gym teachers will be sacked forever and ever,
So abolish gym, it's now or never.

Lauren Dick (13)

SONNET: HORRIBLE HOCKEY

We all run onto a green hockey pitch,
And chase after those little coloured balls.
Running up steep slopes will give you a stitch,
Acting instantly on the teacher's calls.
It's not as if I'll ever score a goal,
Not like the stars who sometimes score hatricks.
One day I swear I'll fall into a hole.
I could play with better balls and tactics.
Is there any point to this awful game?
Why don't the government abolish it?
So hockey will not bring me wealth or fame,
Where is the proof that it helps us get fit?
Surely hockey is the worst sport of all,
Do the teachers like to make us look fools?

Kate Blacker

SONNET: WRITE ONE

I really don't know what on earth to write -
A sonnet doesn't come just straight away.
I'll never get the stupid thing just right;
I really can't - whatever she may say.
A poem isn't meant to be a chore.
My English teacher says she's sure I'll cope.
I think that poetry is just a bore;
For me I know there's really not much hope.
Despite the fact she says I'm capable,
I really struggle just to find a rhyme;
Can't find a rhythm that is suitable;
I think this poem is a waste of time . . .
But look! It's come just like she said it would -
A sonnet and I didn't know I could.

Verity Crosswell (13)

A SONNET: TV

I looked up in the paper what to view,
Then went into the room and switched it on.
To turn it on I threw at it my shoe,
And then I sucked a lemon bon-bon.
The programme I was watching was boring,
My brother argued over what to watch.
In the corner my dad was still snoring,
After he had drunk half a ton of scotch.
My mother came and told us not to shout,
I grabbed the control and said that I'd won.
My brother went off and started to pout,
Now I'm on my own and having no fun.
Dad's snoring so hard it's starting to hurt,
I might as well just do my homework.

Katie Bristow (13)

A Sonnet On Smoking

Why do these people throw their lives away,
As day by day they puff out lethal smoke?
Don't they know that one day they'll have to pay?
Does no one understand - it's not a joke?
One day some may stop - realise what they've done,
Others won't realise until it is too late.
Never stopping to think what they've become,
Their love of smoking has quickened their fate.
And day after day they poison themselves.
Some try, some do not; some die, some do not.
Cast away like bottles stacked up on shelves -
Their true identity has been forgot.
Even though I am just a little child,
I know I will not be so fatally beguiled.

Joanna Dacombe (13)

A QUESTION OF LOVE

Today is the day when ladies may ask,
The men they have loved right from the start,
To agree and say 'I do,' to the task,
Of forever keeping them in their heart.
The women say to the men, 'I love you,'
Expressing exactly how they feel,
Knowing that they will see their marriage through,
And the love between them is for real.
They don't want for their love to still linger,
But to place the sacred wedding ring,
On their partner's lonely and bare finger
And to hear the wedding angels sing.
The love they both feel will last forever
And they shall remain always together.

Gita Dhaliwal (13)

LOVE EVERY LEAP YEAR

So what is a leap year we ask ourselves.
One day, every four years when woman ask
Their only loves to take them for their wives,
She hopes that someday soon they'll share the task,
In uniting their families into one,
So they can spread happiness everywhere.
Maybe, some day she will conceive a son,
Or daughter and vow that they will take care
Of each other. Do you know the meaning
When you discover your undying love,
And get that strong sensational feeling,
That you re flying on wings of a dove?
Now do you understand commitment here?
Your whole life before you, but do not fear.

Naomi Jasmin Clark (12)

SONNET: RUNNING BLUES

My body is screaming no not again!
My heart is pumping, my brow damp with sweat.
Eight laps ahead of me, oh how much pain!
'Come on,' my class mates scream, how I regret
coming to school on this sunny, dry day.
My lungs feel as though they are closing in.
I dream of drink on this morning in May.
My side is in pain as if a huge pin
is riveting my body, as I run.
'Only two more laps.' I cannot do it!
My mum always insists that it is fun.
How easy it would be if I were fit.
The finishing line is coming in sight.
I drop to the ground and out like a light.

Anna Barañski (13)

A Sonnet On Animal Rights

Why do animals have to die for us?
For food, for fur why don't we let them live?
You may wonder why I'm making a fuss;
The right to live is what we all must give.
They could be killed and skinned just for their fur,
Or put to death so we can eat the food
Into their deathly cage they have been lured.
We should not be taught to kill - for our own good.
Would we like it? What do you think we'd say
If we were cooped up in cages for life?
They count what's left of their lives day by day,
Until the time comes when they get the knife.
So next time you wear fur coats or eat meat,
Think of their lives; death - they can never beat.

Sarah Cobbold (12)

SONNET: SPRINGTIME

Under the ground everything is moving,
Growing and pushing, reaching for light,
The trees are growing, taller and sprouting,
Small, sticky buds, green and bright.
First to pop up is the crocus, the snowdrop,
Delicate and dancing swaying in the breeze.
The farmer is outside planting his crops,
Out later is the blossom attracting the bees.
The birds come home waving winter goodbye,
Sitting on the railings preening themselves clean,
Soon will come summer, hot, dusty and dry,
The high tree canopy, yellow and green.
But still here is the spring daffodils galore,
Waiting, just waiting to cover the floor.

Jennifer Cochrane (12)

FISHERMAN'S KNOT

My skull of opalescent white
Commutes the lava ocean bed
Grinning as a phantom might.

The thunder gulls belay their flight
Transformed to bobbing wreaths o'erhead
My skull of opalescent white.

The witch thought sudden loss, a slight
Then broke those flimsy vows invented
Grinning as a phantom might.

My staunch companions eased her plight
Now all her failed discretions tread
My skull of opalescent white.

Could I but stamp on her delight
And stain her counterpane blood red
Grinning as a phantom might.

She'll see one day, by candlelight
Half buried, screaming, by her bed
My skull of opalescent white
Grinning as a phantom might.

Clive W Macdonald

HOW TIME FLIES

Oh how time quickly passes by:
Where do the hours go?
Vanishing it seems with the blink of an eye.

Days, weeks and months now simply fly
Unlike days of long ago:
Oh how time quickly passes by.

Even the clouds in the heavens so high
Seem to rush as I watch from below;
Vanishing it seems with the blink of an eye.

A flower blooms but is soon to die,
Then another one starts to grow;
Oh how time quickly passes by.

The robin he warbles his song 'neath the sky,
Then he's ready for off 'tis the end of the show;
Vanishing it seems with the blink of an eye.

No sooner dusk than the night draws nigh,
One would seem to have the other in tow;
Oh how time quickly passes by,
Vanishing it seems with the blink of an eye.

Vivien Holden

My Exiled Heart

My exiled heart will hide its pain
Lost on a lover's desert isle
Until you turn to me again

You said 'Farewell' with some disdain
Which you may soon regret, meanwhile
My exiled heart will hide its pain

My lone endeavours seem in vain
What can I do that is worthwhile
Until you turn to me again

Because your love was under strain
Fermenting in false rumour's bile
My exiled heart will hide its pain

I'll make pretence that I maintain
An air of nonchalance and style
Until you turn to me again

My love endures and will remain
Despite deceit and jealous guile
My exiled heart will hide its pain
Until you turn to me again

Cyril Mountjoy

HYSTERECTOMY - POEM II

I wish I had not lived to see the day
When I lay butchered on your steel cold bed;
My heaven, with precision, cut away.

A stitched dead-end portending love's decay,
And I, still breathing, left, a living dead,
Only to wish I had not seen the day.

Made in one piece; pink banked, she held at bay,
Anxiety; the world - and all it said,
But heaven's rescinded now; I'm cut away.

My quiet breath's uneven; it's astray,
My heart resounds within my chest like lead.
I wish I had not lived to see the day.

There will be no release. I cannot pray;
Cannot reclaim my life, on which you fed,
As, with precision, you cut my heaven away.

Whither your soul? No whither and no way.
Whither all souls who mock the gifts of God?
I wish I had not lived to see the day
When, with precision, you cut my heaven away.

Marilyn Lewis

A PILE OF FROGS SONNET

Frogs in a pile are spawning,
They seem rather odd that way,
They start first thing in the morning,
And croak all the live long day:
'Ribbit,' they seem to be saying,
Piled up like a totem pole,
It's a mating game they're playing,
To fill up the water hole,
With tiny legless tadpoles,
Which bite each other's tails,
They've got to eat somebody,
So thank gord they're not whales:
Our pond will soon be brimming
With small delinquent frogs,
That soon learn the art of swimming,
And jumping onto logs:
Out of 1000 tadpoles, you might find nine or ten
Will survive all through next winter and pile up in a pile next spring.

Mick Nash

TREES IN WINTER

The leaves have all blown off the trees
So every tree looks bald and bare;
They have succumbed to wind and breeze.

Skeletal branches dance to please,
A thousand forks sway in the air;
The leaves have all blown off the trees.

Their coat of autumn foliage flees,
Orange-tanned leaves are now not there;
They have succumbed to wind and breeze.

We hear the howling wild winds tease,
Blasting aloft soil's withered fare;
The leaves have all blown off the trees.

Advent of welcome spring will please
New shoots in restoration's care;
Winter will fall upon its knees.

The forest sighs and starts to freeze;
East and west winds their booty share:
The leaves have all blown off the trees,
They have succumbed to wind and breeze.

Christine Macleod

A Cheval

Oh to fly across the Seven Seas
Not by plane that I deny
On a winged horse called Pegasus

I want to ride with the wind so free
On a winged horse that flies
Oh to fly across the Seven Seas

To pass above the mountains free
To fly and ride the heavenly skies
On a winged horse called Pegasus

Over hills, dales and lea
To pass the rainbows endless nigh
Oh to fly across the Seven Seas

Tho a dream it may only be
I'll catch it as it's passing by
On a winged horse called Pegasus

If all dreams are a fallacy
I wish to die before I wake to cry
Oh to fly across the Seven Seas
On a winged horse called Pegasus

A B Lawson

DEAR ONE

Dear One, throughout all the years,
I have loved you constantly,
Whether laughing or in tears.

You have shared my doubts and fears
Knowing my heart completely,
Dear One, throughout all the years.

You have been my eyes and ears,
When sense or reason failed me,
Whether laughing or in tears.

Cruising smoothly, grinding gears,
We've travelled on our journey,
Dear One, throughout all the years.

Whichever path our life steers,
I will need your company,
Whether laughing or in tears.

As our winter season nears,
Together we will always be
Dear One, throughout all the years,
Whether laughing or in tears.

Janet Hewitt

YOU ARE

You are my diamond in the light
You are my ruby glowing red
You are my flame that's burning bright
You are the silk upon my bed

You are my stone that's made of gold
You are my emerald shining green
You are the one I need to hold
The most precious thing I have seen

Yes it's you who's my precious jewel
You are my sapphire so blue
My love pool, sparkly and cool
All things beautiful that is you

All things special that I can see
Is everything you are to me

Paul McIntyre

OUTCASTS

In my young days we lived in a blue fug,
Tobacco smoke around us day and night,
Without a cigarette we felt a mug,
In buses, pubs and dance halls it felt right.

Later they told us we had all been fools,
The reeking tubes were leading us to death,
Cigarette manufacturers were ghouls,
Not caring if their profits stilled our breath.

Now smokers have become an outlaw breed,
Huddled in corners outside office doors,
We're better off without the pungent weed,
Although we're plagued by anti-smoking bores.

There is truth in the message that they give,
But should they tell the outcasts how to live?

Peter Hicks

PERSPECTIVE

That Nature mirrors art is quite as true -
In play-back life from screen and page observed -
As it corollary is. We take our cue
From scripts; by fantasies our course is served.
That Nature mirrors Nature is more strange -
Sometimes in miniature - the fractile flower
Mirrors the cliff, while the reflecting range
Of universe expands this mirror-power.
When Science splits the glass, staples the quark
Inside the inside the inside of atom cell,
Then from the double light or double dark
Comes revelation Art cannot dispel.
While in these multi-mirrors Mimic reigns
Perception proffers, Mystery abstains.

Brenda Elder

MALHAM COVE

Round Malham the long walls are greener now,
Greener with the delicate shoots of spring,
Dreamier with the feathered throats that sing.
Would that we were there wandering just now,
By the wooded lanes and low scented bough
That ramble, twisting and turning to bring
Our loitering feet. But swift time is awing,
And haste we to our heaven, I and Thou.
Of God's secret places, this lovely land,
The epitome of an exquisite dream,
And of these dreams, its just before the dawn,
The veil is raised, when fore the Cove we stand,
Surely the creators transcendent beam,
Shone here when enigmatic earth was born.

R E Fairclough

SATURDAY ARTS WORKSHOP

The children act their charming little plays
In groups of five, illustrating a theme,
And as they act their wily, winsome ways
Have the effect of some strange, beauteous dream.
When one group have performed their little act
The other children commentate on it;
It's been agreed amongst them, in a pact,
There shall be praise as well as salty wit,
For each enactment has its things of worth,
As with their freshness 'tcould not fail to do;
Constructive comment can give comely birth
To feats of prowess all of us to woo.
After each group has fitted in its slot
We choose the best performance of the lot.

Tony Dixon

THE ONE WHO KNOWS DOESN'T SPEAK

The one who knows doesn't speak: There's no need.
His wisdom is golden, he knows his place.
He shows one prominent, reflective face,
He's planted his sacred, glowing life seed.
The pieces of nature's puzzle show greed.
The twisted bramble, to his charms embrace
We're blown by this elementary grace.
To his charm and valour, we must take heed.

Hyperion rides high, as dreams crumble,
See what's beneath the frosty, concealed glare.
Through murmuring trees, he once did fumble,
Encompass all amidst his deadly stare.
He sees clearly through, all else he'll humble,
See the fruits in his stream, he now does bare.

Simon Cardy

DENOUEMENT

He has a life it's better not to see
That starts at dark like nightmare's silent screams
But soon will change from all life's meant to be
Destroying in its wake both hopes and dreams
With unsafe sex and popping pills galore
And alcohol to face the dreaded dawning -
Rejection now of all that went before,
While disillusion haunts the morning.

It's harder now to live two lives in one
And soon he'll have to choose which way he'll go
And then the masquerading will be done
So all his friends and colleagues then will know
That he, the slick chameleon, is gone -
Become the vole that day or light will shun.

Linda McIntyre

TO YOU

I love you with my hands that touch your face.
I love you with my lips that cling to thine.
I love you with my blood that flows as wine
Through all my being, and if I could trace
Upon the darkened moments of his place,
My map of love for you, then how each line
Of sapphire, gold, and crimson would entwine
About your beauty, and abounding grace.

I love you every hour of every day,
And every moment of those yearning hours
The flame that burns, burns brighter yet, and deep
Through the dim twilight and the shadowy grey
Of what I wander in, I see the towers
Of love's clear shining city that you keep.

W H Lunn

THEATRE OF DREAMS

You were right, the lead's a better stayer:
a weak imitating understudy,
the director's sure I am no player,
hidden in the wings all slashed and bloody.

You were right, exacting your impression:
knives are like that in the way of butter,
liars make less classic their confession
restricting the heart to a mere utter.

You were right, audience demands return:
although it's possible I've misconceived
of this timeless place in which I sojourn,
adoration denied becomes bereaved.

In this theatre of dreams, without a cast,
can a future be derived from the past?

Tony Downing